MORE THAN A

MILLION MENUS

LINDA DOESER began her publishing career with the cookery partwork *Supercook* in the early 1970s, and since then has edited and contributed to numerous books and magazines. She is the author of several books, including *Cooking Under Pressure, The Budget Book, Cocktails and Party Drinks, The Complete Book of Desserts, The Little Green Avocado Book* and *1,000 Healthy Eating Recipes.* A number of her books have been published in the U.S. and translated into several European languages. An enthusiastic traveller, she enjoys trying new foods and foreign dishes. She lives with her daughter, dog and cat in London.

More than a Million Menus

Edited by
Linda Doeser

Kerstin Wachtmeister
Photography: Kjell Nilsson

PRC

Written by Kerstin Wachtmeister
Home economist Birgitta Lindqvist
Photography by Kjell Nilsson
Translated by Barbro Magnusson
Translation assistant Paddy Cutts
Edited by Linda Doeser

Published by Sunburst Books, Deacon House,
65 Old Church Street, London SW3 5BS.

ISBN 1 85648 062 3

Printed in Hong Kong

FOREWORD

Does anyone need another cook book? Food lovers and keen cooks - you and I know that there are never enough cookery books, at least not on our shelves. Cookery books can be a real source of pleasure, but I don't think I would have ever had the idea of writing one if the publishers had not produced this very good plan with three separate flip-over parts.
Being able to turn the pages back and forth for different meals and combinations and looking at how the different combinations work and suit each other inspired me.

Will it be enough? Do the different courses go together well? What about the dessert? How about the combinations of taste and colour? Will I be able to get everything done in time? These are the sorts of questions all cooks ask themselves when planning a meal, whether for big parties or for family dinners. With this cookery book, I hope that the planning will be much easier - and more fun.

When I had made up my mind to write this book, I started to look in folders and piles of papers. I have been interested in food for as long as I can remember, reading and collecting recipes from books, newspapers, magazines and many other sources. I have tried to select the best from my collection in this book. Included here are hints and recipes from famous hoteliers, restaurants, chefs, food writers and other experts and professionals. Good friends, relations and colleagues have also contributed, as well as my fantastic fishmonger and my unusually knowledgeable Austrian butcher. I have brought recipes back from my travels, too. Often, I have had only the impression and memory of a dish and have then tried to re-create it in my own kitchen.

Foto: Holger Edström

As with any food lover's collection, there are both party recipes and basic meals in my book. There are more dishes for entertaining for than day-to-day dinners, but with a good cookery book, one should be able to combine and create one's own menus from the original ideas.

Many of the recipes are Swedish. Many others have been inspired by Southern European and French cooking but not *nouvelle cuisine*. These recipes are not for the health conscious or for slimmers. My recipes are probably better for the soul than the body!

Many dishes are classics, which you will probably recognize, but I hope they have a bit more flair than the traditional recipes. This may be the result of modern preparation techniques and more gentle handling. I also include recipes that I hope you will find a source of new inspiration. In the desserts section, especially, you will probably find much you have not seen before. I have often taken a standard recipe as a starting point, begun to experiment while cooking, and then all of a sudden a new dish has been created.

Together with Birgitta Lindqvist, the home economist who worked on this book with me, I have made and tasted every dish. Now, I hope that what has given my friends and me pleasure and satisfied our appetites will also inspire you and give pleasure to your friends, because food is at its best when shared with others. Good luck with choosing the menus in your new cookery book.

GLANCE THROUGH THESE PAGES TO FIND YOUR MENU

YOU CAN SEE IMMEDIATELY WHETHER THE RECIPES GO TOGETHER

This book is divided into three parts: 100 starters, 100 main courses and 100 desserts. You can combine them in more than one million different ways. In this unique book you can look at each part separately and then easily combine the various alternatives to see how the recipes suit each other, which ingredients are required, and how much of every recipe can be made in advance.

For ease and simplicity, all the recipes are numbered: starters from 100-199, main courses 200-299 and desserts 300-399. Of course, not all the dishes can be combined as some will not go well together, but with a little thought, you can put together the most delicious menus for two, three or more courses – even an inviting buffet. Just remember that all the dishes should be in harmony when it comes to taste, colour, shape and texture.

YOU WILL QUICKLY FIND OUT ALL YOU NEED TO KNOW

Every dish is illustrated with a colour photograph and has detailed cooking instructions. In addition, there are suggestions and variations, ideas for accompaniments, and recommended drinks. Most suggestions for what to drink are classic, but some are unconventional and may be a surprise. Do try them out. You will find three very practical boxes on the page beside each photograph. These detail the level of difficulty, the preparation time and whether the dish can be made in advance. There are four levels of difficulty: easy, fairly easy, medium difficult and difficult. The preparation time refers only to the working time. Times for marinating, freezing, chilling etc. are usually included separately. Always read the recipe all the way through before starting. Do not feel tied to a recipe headed 'main course' or 'starter'; it is often only a question of quantity.

LEVEL OF DIFFICULTY easy
PREPARATION TIME 1 hr + freezing time
PREPARE IN ADVANCE yes

YOU CAN SEE AT A GLANCE HOW MUCH CAN BE MADE IN ADVANCE

How much of the recipe can be prepared in advance is clear, as the relevant instruction numbers are printed in bold type. This is an invaluable aid if you are going to make more than one dish and you wish to do as much preparation as possible before your guests arrive.

ACCOMPANIMENTS AND MENU SUGGESTIONS

At the back of the book there is a separate section that includes several basic recipes, numbered 400-443. Accompaniments include vegetables, sauces, pickles etc. Some main course recipes occasionally refer to this section at the back of the book. There are also several suggestions for menus and a detailed index which will help you to find things in this book easily. As you can see, More Than A Million Menus will offer you undreamed of opportunities.

CONTENTS

SOUPS & STARTERS

MAIN COURSES

PUDDINGS & DESSERTS

ACCOMPANIMENTS

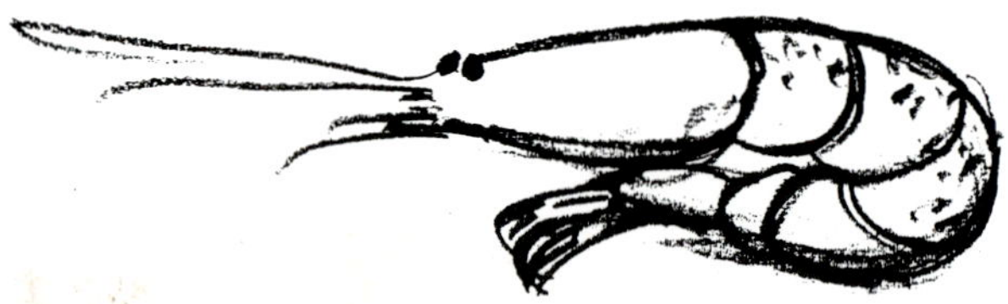

ACCOMPANIMENTS

400 GRILLING TIMES AND MARINADES

MARINADE FOR MEAT

for 1 kg/2¼ lb meat:
50 ml/2 fl oz sherry, blackcurrant juice, vinegar or wine
50 ml/2 fl oz vegetable oil
50 ml/2 fl oz soya sauce
juice of ½ lemon
½ tsp freshly ground black pepper
1 clove garlic, crushed (optional)
½ tsp ground ginger (for pork)

Mix all the ingredients for the marinade. Place the meat in a bowl and pour over the marinade. Allow approximately 30 minutes for sliced or cubed meat to marinate and 2-3 hours for joints and large cuts.

MARINADE FOR FISH

150 ml/5 fl oz vegetable oil
50 ml/2 fl oz lemon juice
50 ml/2 fl oz chili sauce
1 small red onion, sliced
½-1 tsp black pepper
a little tabasco sauce

GRILLING TIMES FOR MEAT

MEAT TYPE	THICKNESS	COOKING TIME
BEEF		
Entrecôte	15 mm/½ inch	2-3 minutes each side (medium)
Grill slice (cheapest cut)	15 mm/½ inch	3-4 minutes each side (medium)
Grill slice (roast beef)	15 mm/½ inch	3-4 minutes each side (medium)
Rump steak (very thin)	5 mm/¼ inch	2 minutes grill only one side
Hamburger	1 cm/⅓ inch	approximately 2 minutes each side
PORK		
Chops or cutlets	15 mm/½ inch	3-4 minutes each side
Ribs	1 cm/⅓ inch	4-5 minutes each side
Ham	15 mm/½ inch	3 minutes each side
Spare ribs (thick cut)		15 minutes each side
Pork steaks	3-4 cm/1-1½ inches	15 minutes each side
LAMB		
Chops or cutlets	15 mm/½ inch	2-2½ minutes each side (medium)
Sliced steak	15 mm/½ inch	3-4 minutes each side (medium)
Breast		4-5 minutes each side
SAUSAGES		
Bratwurst		approximately 8 minutes in total
Long thick smoked sausage	15 mm/½ inch	approximately 2 minutes each side
Breakfast sausage		approximately 8 minutes in total
Frankfurter		approximately 4 minutes in total

These times are suitable for barbecues and gas grills. Add a few extra minutes for electric grills. However, you should remember that it is the heat and the distance from the heat that decide the times. When cooking on the barbecue, thicker meat pieces and meat on the bone should be placed further from the charcoal.

All these grilling times are approximate; it is not possible to give exact times. When the meat is ready, it should be a beautiful golden brown colour on the outside. Beef or lamb should be pink or red inside, and pork should be cooked all through.

Turn the meat when it starts to 'sweat' on the top side. When pink juice starts to ooze out, the meat will be pink inside. Continue grilling if you want the meat to be well done. A simple way of testing if the meat is ready is to use a sharp knife to cut a little slice in the edge.

Meat for grilling should be tender and not too lean. It is easier to grill sliced meat, such as entrecôtes, ham, chops, and lamb cutlets. It will have the best colour if it is at room temperature when you start cooking it. Remove it from the refrigerator 30 minutes before grilling. If you are cooking the meat straight from the refrigerator, add 1-2 extra minutes to the grilling time for sliced meat. Frozen meat should be fully thawed.

Marinating the meat is a good way to flavour it. The meat will then have extra taste. Try to avoid high heat while grilling. Burned food is neither tasty nor healthy. It is, therefore, important to grill over embers when barbecuing, and never over an open fire or with fuel which is not intended for cooking.

GRILLING TIMES FOR FISH

FISH TYPE	THICKNESS	COOKING TIME
Salmon	15 mm/½ inch	4-5 minutes each side
Halibut	15 mm/½ inch	approximately 7 minutes each side
Herring	filleted	3 minutes each side
Perch	whole, gutted	3 minutes each side
Cod fillet (in foil parcel)		15-20 minutes
Mackerel, Rainbow trout etc. (in foil)		15-20 minutes
Fish kebabs		3 minutes each side

Fish should be grilled at a high temperature. Use only a small amount of oil or no oil at all. Oily fish, such as herring, mackerel, sea bass, rainbow trout, salmon and eel, are best suited to grilling. You do not have to remove the backbone from small fish but they should be split. You can, of course, also remove the backbone and grill the fish opened up. Large fish are best grilled in slices or fillets.

Fish that are to be grilled may be marinated. Use the marinade for basting the fish pieces. If the fish are to be placed on the wire rack, brush the rack with a little oil to prevent the skin from sticking. Fish can also be grilled seasoned with herbs and spices in a foil parcel.

401 BROCCOLI TIMBALES

Serves 4

250 g/8¾ oz broccoli
salt
100 ml/3½ fl oz crème fraîche
2 eggs, lightly beaten
herb salt
freshly ground white pepper
1 carrot
1 tbsp butter

Boil the broccoli in lightly salted water for 15-20 minutes. Drain and allow to cool slightly. Cut it into smaller pieces and purée in a mixer or food processor. Pour the purée back into the saucepan. Mix in the crème fraîche and eggs. Season with salt or herb salt and white pepper to taste. Thinly slice the carrot. Preheat the oven to 200° C/400° F, gas mark 6. Grease small timbale moulds or ovenproof ramekins with the butter and place one carrot slice in the base of each mould. Pour the purée into the moulds, leaving a space of about 20 mm/¾ inch at the top. Place the moulds in a roasting tin half filled with hot water and bake for 20-25 minutes or until the timbales have risen.

402 PICKLED FRESH CUCUMBER
Serves 4

200 g/7 oz fresh cucumber

Marinade:
1 tbsp sugar
1 tbsp vinegar
5 tbsp water
1 tsp salt
white pepper
1 tbsp finely chopped parsley

Rinse but do not peel the cucumber. Thinly slice and place in a bowl. Mix the marinade ingredients and pour over the cucumber. Sprinkle over the parsley. Set aside for a couple of hours before serving.

403 CUCUMBER SALAD WITH HAZELNUTS
Serves 4

1 green cucumber
100 ml/3½ fl oz sour cream
50 g/1¾ oz hazelnuts, finely chopped
1 tbsp grated horseradish
herb salt

Mix together the nuts, horseradish and sour cream. Set aside for 30 minutes. Season with the herb salt. Cut the cucumber into thin slices or strips and place them in a bowl. Pour over the sauce just before serving.

404 PILAU RICE
Serves 4

2 tbsp butter or vegetable oil
½ onion, finely chopped
260 g/9 oz long grain rice
600 ml/1 pint water or bouillon
½ tsp salt

Heat the butter or oil in a saucepan and sauté the onion. Add the rice and fry for 2-3 minutes until it is white. Add the water or bouillon and salt. Bring to the boil, reduce the heat, cover and simmer, without stirring, for 18 minutes.

405 POMMES CHÂTEAUX
Serves 4

10-12 potatoes, cut into wedges
water
2-3 tbsp butter

Preheat the oven to 220° C/425° F, gas mark 7. Place the potatoes in boiling water and allow to boil for 3 minutes. Drain and allow the steam to evaporate. Melt the butter in an ovenproof pan. Add the potatoes and coat with the butter. Roast the potatoes, turning once, for 20 minutes until soft and golden.

406 DUCHESSE POTATOES
Serves 4

8-10 medium potatoes
2 tbsp butter
2 egg yolks
salt
freshly ground white pepper

Boil the potatoes in unsalted water until soft. Drain, mash, add the butter and egg yolks and mix well. Season with salt and white pepper to taste. This purée can be used for piping or can be spooned around fish or meat dishes to be browned with a cheese topping. It can also be piped into roses or stars on a greased baking sheet. Bake at 250° C/500° F, gas mark 10, for 5-10 minutes or until golden brown. Serve the potato roses with fried meat dishes or fried poultry.

407 GOLDEN MASHED POTATOES
Serves 4

1 kg/2¼ lb potatoes, cut into pieces
150 ml/5 fl oz milk
salt
freshly ground white pepper
2 tsp butter
150 ml/5 fl oz double cream
130 g/4½ oz Gruyère or Emmental cheese, grated

Boil the potatoes in unsalted water until soft. Mash with a potato masher or fork. Bring the milk to the boil and add to the mashed potato until smooth. Season with salt and pepper to taste. Preheat the oven to 220° C/425° F, gas mark 7. Grease an ovenproof dish with the butter and fill with the mashed potato. Smooth the surface and pour a 1-cm/¼-inch thick layer of cream on top. Cover with grated cheese and bake until the surface is golden brown and crunchy. The mashed potato can be made well in advance and kept in the refrigerator. Pour over the cream and sprinkle over the grated cheese just before baking, which will then take a little longer, approximately 30 minutes.

408 HASSELBACK POTATOES
Serves 4

3-4 tbsp butter, melted
10-12 potatoes
1½ tsp salt
1 tbsp breadcrumbs
2 tbsp grated cheese

Grease an ovenproof dish with a little of the butter. Preheat the oven to 220° C/425° F, gas mark 7. Cut the potatoes into thin slices about three-quarters of the way through. Each potato should be held together by its base. Place the potato, sliced side up, on the prepared dish.

Brush with melted butter, season with salt and roast in the oven for 20 minutes, basting with butter once or twice. Sprinkle over the breadcrumbs and grated cheese and roast for a further 15-20 minutes until soft and golden. .

409 BAKED CHEESE GRATINÉE POTATOES

Serves 4

1 kg/2¼ lb large potatoes
3 tbsp butter
salt
freshly ground white pepper
120 g/4 oz Gruyère or Emmental cheese, grated

Preheat the oven to 220° C/425° F, gas mark 7. Grease a large ovenproof dish with 1 tbsp of the butter. Cut the potatoes into slices all the way through, but keeping the slices in position so that the potatoes look whole. As each potato is cut, place it in the dish quite close to the others and press down so that the slices fan out slightly. Baste with the butter and season with salt and white pepper. Bake in the oven for approximately 15 minutes. Sprinkle over the grated cheese and baste the potatoes with butter. Bake for a further 20-30 minutes until the potatoes are soft inside and golden and crunchy on the outside.

410 ROSTI POTATOES

Serves 4

6-8 potatoes (600-700 g/1¼-1½ lb)
butter

Roughly grate or cut the potatoes into fine strips. Drain. Melt some butter in a skillet or frying-pan and add a spoonful of the grated potatoes. Pat down with a spatula and fry the rosti on both sides until the potato is thoroughly cooked and golden. Keep warm while you fry the remaining rosti in the same way

411 POTATO GRATIN

Serves 4

1 kg/2¼ lb potatoes, sliced
1 tbsp butter
salt
2 cloves garlic, crushed
200 ml/7 fl oz double cream

Preheat the oven to 200° C/400° F, gas mark 6. Grease an ovenproof dish with the butter. Arrange the potatoes slices in layers in it, seasoning each layer with salt. Mix the cream and garlic and pour over the potatoes. Bake in the oven for approximately 40 minutes.

412 POTATO CROQUETTES

Serves 4

8-10 medium potatoes
2 tbsp butter
2 egg yolks
salt
freshly ground white pepper
1 egg, lightly beaten
120 g/4 oz breadcrumbs
50 ml/2 fl oz vegetable oil

Boil the potatoes in unsalted water until soft. Drain and mash. Beat in the butter and egg yolk and season with salt and pepper. Shape the purée into rolls or balls. Coat the with beaten egg and then breadcrumbs. Heat the oil and fry or deep-fry them until golden.

ALMOND COVERED POTATO CROQUETTES

Coat the croquettes in chopped or flaked almonds, instead of breadcrumbs, before frying or deep-frying.

413 LAYERED POTATOES

Serves 6

1 kg/2¼ lb potatoes
1 small swede
1 carrot
salt
1 x 250 g/8¾ oz pkt frozen chopped spinach, thawed
150-200 ml/5-7 fl oz milk
1½ tbsp butter
freshly ground pepper
50-100 ml/2-3½ fl oz double cream
60-85 g/2-3 oz Gruyère or Emmental cheese, grated

Cut the potatoes, swede and carrot into pieces. Boil the potatoes separately in unsalted water until soft. Boil the swede and carrot together in lightly salted water. Squeeze the water from the spinach. Drain and mash the potatoes with 1 tbsp of the butter. Beat in the milk until smooth and airy. Purée the swede and carrot in a food processor or by rubbing through a wire strainer. Mix the purée with one-third of the mashed potato. Mix the spinach with 6 tbsp mashed potato. Grease an ovenproof glass dish with the butter. Place the orange-coloured purée in the base, cover with the green purée and top with mashed potatoes. (This can all be done in advance.) Preheat the oven to 180° C/350° F, gas mark 4. Whip the cream and mix with the grated cheese. Bake the layered potatoes for 15 minutes. Remove the dish from the oven and spread the cream and cheese mixture over the top. Return to the oven and bake for a further 15 minutes, or until the mash is thoroughly heated.

414 BAKED VEGETABLES
Serves 4

5 potatoes
3 carrots
150 g/5¼ oz celery sticks
2 small parsnips
2 tsp butter
300 ml/10 fl oz double cream
100 ml/3½ fl oz milk
1 clove garlic, crushed
salt
freshly ground white pepper

Preheat the oven to 170° C/325° F, gas mark 3. Peel the root vegetables and cut all the vegetables into strips. Grease an ovenproof dish with the butter. Place the vegetables in the dish. Mix together the cream, milk and garlic and season with salt and pepper to taste. Pour over the vegetables and bake for 50-60 minutes. Add more cream or milk if necessary.

415 CELERIAC PURÉE
Serves 4

1 large celeriac root
1 tsp lemon juice
50-100 ml/2-3½ fl oz double cream or crème fraîche
1 tbsp water
herb salt
freshly ground white pepper

Peel and dice the celeriac and place in cold water with the lemon juice to prevent discoloration. Bring a little water to the boil in a saucepan, add the celeriac and boil until the pieces are soft enough to mash and most of the water has been absorbed. Purée the celeriac in a food processor or by rubbing it through a wire strainer. Return it to the saucepan, stir in the butter and add the cream or crème fraîche. Season with salt or herb salt and white pepper to taste.

416 GRANDMA'S CUCUMBER

4 kg/8¾ lb cucumber
salt
blackcurrant leaves
cherry leaves
mustard seeds
dill sprigs
dried red chilis, broken in pieces

Marinade:
600 ml/1 pint water
700 ml/1¼ pints vinegar
4 tbsp white sugar
1 tsp cream of tartar

Peel the cucumbers and cut them in half lengthwise. Scrape out the seeds and cut the halves in the middle. Rub with plenty of salt and set aside overnight to dégorge. Drain the cucumbers and dry on kitchen paper. To make the marinade, bring the water and vinegar to the boil and add the sugar and cream of tartar. Make layers of cucumber, blackcurrant leaves, cherry leaves, mustard seeds, dill and chilis in a heatproof glass jar. Pour over the boiling marinade to cover the cucumbers entirely. Cover the jar with a towel and keep in a cool place. After 3 weeks the cucumbers will be ready. They will keep for a long time if the marinade always covers them.

417 ROWANBERRY JAM

1 kg/2¼ lb rowanberries, preferably frostbitten
1.25 kg/2¾ lb sugar
300 ml/10 fl oz water
100 ml/3½ fl oz brandy (optional)

Pick over and rinse the rowanberries. (Allow to dry and place on a tray in the freezer if they were picked before the frost arrived.) Boil the water and sugar, stirring until the sugar has dissolved. Add the berries and simmer very slowly until they are soft, clear and a beautiful colour. They should not be too mushy. Shake the pan from time to time to distribute them evenly. Skim thoroughly. Remove the saucepan from the heat and stir in the brandy, if using. Pour the warm jam into small jars, cover with greaseproof discs and seal with lids or jam covers.

418 LINGONBERRY OR CRANBERRY SAUCE

2.5 kg/5½ lb lingonberries or cranberries
1 litre/1¾ pints water
2 kg/4½ lb sugar

Pick over and rinse the berries. Bring the water to the boil, add the berries and cook for 10 minutes. Skim the surface. Remove from the heat and add the sugar. Stir until it has dissolved and the mixture has thickened. Pour the sauce into clean jars, cover with greaseproof paper discs and seal with lids or jam covers.

RAW STIRRED LINGONBERRY OR CRANBERRY SAUCE

2.5 kg/5½ lb lingonberries or cranberries
1.5-2 kg/3¼-4½ lb sugar

Pick over and rinse the berries and place them in an earthenware or china bowl. Add the sugar and stir with a wooden spoon for approximately 1 hour or until the sugar has fully dissolved and the berries are mashed. The sauce can also be made in a food processor, which is much faster. Pour the sauce into jars, cover with greaseproof paper discs and seal with lids or jam covers.

419 BÉARNAISE SAUCE
Serves 4

150-200 g/5¼-7 oz butter
1 tbsp finely chopped shallots
5-6 white peppercorns, crushed
2 parsley sprigs
1 tsp dried tarragon
2 tbsp vinegar
4 tbsp water
3 egg yolks
3 tbsp finely chopped parsley
salt
freshly ground white pepper

Melt the butter and set aside to clarify. Place the shallots, peppercorns, parsley sprigs, tarragon, vinegar and water in a saucepan and bring to the boil. Boil until reduced by more than half. Place the egg yolks in a heatproof bowl. Strain the boiled liquid into them, beating constantly. Set the bowl over a pan of hot but not boiling water. Beat until the mixture is thick and airy. Remove from the heat and beat in the butter, a little at a time. Do not add the residue from the base of the saucepan. Add the chopped parsley and season with salt, pepper and tarragon.

420 MUSHROOM SAUCE
Serves 4

1 tbsp butter
2 shallots, finely chopped
200 g/7 oz mushrooms, sliced
100 ml/3½ fl oz bouillon or light stock
1-2 tbsp ruby port
200 ml/7 fl oz double cream or crème fraîche
salt
freshly ground white pepper

Melt the butter and sauté the shallots over low heat until soft. Add the mushrooms and cook, stirring. Add the bouillon or stock and the port and simmer for 2-3 minutes. Add the cream or crème fraîche and simmer, stirring constantly, until the sauce has the desired consistency. Season with salt and white pepper to taste.

421 CUMBERLAND SAUCE
Serves 4

peel of ½ orange
peel of ½ lemon
150 ml/5 fl oz water
2½ tbsp redcurrant jelly
3 tbsp port
3 tbsp red wine
1-2 tbsp French mustard
juice of 1 orange
salt
freshly ground white pepper

Thinly pare the rind of the orange and lemon. Cut into very thin, strips. Bring the water to the boil and boil the peel for a few minutes. Drain. Stir together the redcurrant jelly, port, wine, mustard and orange juice over low heat. Season with salt and pepper to taste. Add the strips of peel and set the sauce aside to cool.

422 HOLLANDAISE SAUCE
Serves 4

150-200 g/5¼-7 oz butter
3 egg yolks
2 tbsp water or dry white wine
juice of 1 lemon
freshly ground white pepper
salt
cayenne pepper or paprika

Melt the butter over low heat and set aside. Place the egg yolks and water or wine in a heatproof bowl and set over a pan of hot, but not boiling water. Beat vigorously until the mixture is thick and airy. Remove from the heat and beat in the butter, a little at a time. Add the lemon juice and salt, white pepper and cayenne or paprika to taste.

423 GRAVAD LAX SAUCE
Serves 4-6

3 tbsp Swedish mustard
200 ml/7 fl oz oil
1 large bunch dill
salt
freshly ground white pepper

Fit the metal blade in the food processor. Add the mustard, start the processor and drizzle in the oil in a fine stream. Stop the processor. Roughly chop the dill; do not remove the rough stalks. Place the dill in the processor, switch on and work until the dill is finely chopped. Season with salt and pepper to taste. Also see recipe 206.

424 SUPREME GRAVAD LAX SAUCE
Serves 4-6

150 ml/5 fl oz mayonnaise (see recipe 426)
100 ml/3½ fl oz sour cream
2 tbsp mustard
2½ tbsp French mustard
freshly ground black pepper
6 tbsp finely chopped dill

Beat all the ingredients together to make a milder, less sweet sauce which is also well suited to serving with boiled crab.

425 FLAVOURED BUTTERS

ANCHOVY BUTTER
100 g/3½ oz butter, softened
6 anchovy fillets, chopped
freshly ground white pepper
1 tsp finely chopped onion

DILL BUTTER
100 g/3½ oz butter, softened
2 tbsp finely chopped dill
½ tsp lemon juice
freshly ground black pepper

PEPPER BUTTER
100 g/3½ oz butter, softened
freshly ground white pepper
paprika
2 tbsp finely chopped red pepper
1 tsp tomato purée

HORSERADISH BUTTER
100 g/3½ oz butter, softened
2 tbsp freshly grated horseradish

PARSLEY BUTTER
100 g/3½ oz butter, softened
freshly ground black pepper
3 tbsp finely chopped parsley
½ tsp lemon juice

GARLIC BUTTER
100 g/3½ oz butter, softened
white pepper
2 cloves garlic, crushed

HERB FARM BUTTER
100 g/3½ oz butter, softened
freshly ground black pepper
1 tbsp finely chopped parsley
1 tbsp finely chopped dill
½ tbsp finely chopped chives
½ tbsp finely chopped cress
½ tsp dried tarragon

Beat the butter, add the remaining ingredients and mix thoroughly. Shape into a roll and wrap in foil or greaseproof paper. Place in the refrigerator to harden. Cut into slices just before serving. Each recipe gives approximately 10 slices.

426 MAYONNAISE
approximately 400 ml/14 fl oz

2 egg yolks
1 tbsp vinegar
½ tsp salt
freshly ground white pepper
cayenne pepper
1 tsp French mustard
350-400 ml/12-14 fl oz vegetable oil

All the ingredients should be at the same temperature. Mix together the egg yolks, vinegar, salt, pepper and mustard. Beat with an electric whisk, wooden spoon or fork, adding the oil, first drop by drop and then in a fine stream as the mixture thickens. It should be thick, shiny and smooth. Add cayenne pepper to taste. Season with salt and pepper and add a little lemon juice if required. If the mayonnaise curdles, place an egg yolk in a clean bowl and stir in the curdled mayonnaise, little by little.

427 CHILI MAYONNAISE WITH HORSERADISH
Serves 3-4

200 ml/7 fl oz mayonnaise
(see recipe 426)
1½ tbsp chili sauce
1 tbsp grated horseradish

Mix the ingredients together and serve with shellfish or shellfish salad.

428 RHODE ISLAND DRESSING
Serves 4

½ clove garlic, halved
150 ml/5 fl oz mayonnaise (see recipe 426)
50 ml/2 fl oz sour cream
1½ tbsp tomato purée or chili sauce
1 tbsp dry sherry or brandy
few drops tabasco sauce
salt

Rub the bowl with the cut side of the garlic clove. Mix all the ingredients together and stir until the sauce is smooth.

429 GREEN SAUCE
Serves 4

200 ml/7 fl oz mayonnaise (see recipe 426)
1 tbsp finely chopped parboiled spinach
1 tbsp finely chopped dill
1 tbsp finely chopped parsley
1 tbsp finely chopped chervil
1 tbsp finely cut chives
1 tbsp finely chopped fresh tarragon or
1 tsp dried tarragon
1 clove garlic, crushed

Mix the mayonnaise with the spinach and herbs. Add a little crushed garlic, if liked. Serve with smoked or boiled cold fish, fish or shellfish pâtés.

430 MANGO SAUCE
Serves 4

1-2 ripe mangoes
salt
grated ginger

Cut the mango in half around the stone, peel and dice the flesh. Cut away the flesh remaining on the stone. Purée by rubbing through a wire strainer or in a food processor. Add a little water, if necessary. Season with salt and ginger to taste. This goes well with farmhouse pâté, smoked meats and ham.

431 NOBI SAUCE
Serves 10

2 eggs
2 tbsp red wine vinegar
500 ml/17 fl oz oil
1 tsp salt

freshly ground black pepper
$2^1/_2$ tsp French mustard
1 clove garlic, crushed
2 tbsp finely chopped chives

Place the eggs in boiling water and boil for exactly 3 minutes. Crack and scrape out the contents into the bowl of a food processor fitted with a plastic blade. Work until the eggs are mashed. Add the vinegar and oil alternately through the tube while the processor is working. The sauce should be as thick as mayonnaise. Season with salt, pepper, mustard, garlic and chives to taste. Set aside to infuse for at least 30 minutes before serving. Nobi sauce can be made well in advance and kept in a screwtop jar.

432 WHITE WINE SAUCE
Serves 4

3 tbsp butter
1 shallot, finely chopped
150 ml/5 fl oz dry white wine
1 fish stock cube
500 ml/17 fl oz whipping cream
1 tbsp flour
juice of 1 lemon
salt
cayenne pepper or tabasco sauce

Melt 1 tbsp of the butter and sauté the onion for 2-3 minutes. Add the wine and stock cube and boil until reduced by half. Cream together half the remaining butter and the flour to make a *beurre manié*. Add the cream to the sauce, a little at a time, beating constantly. Beat in the *beurre manié*, a little at a time. Simmer for approximately 10 minutes until thick and smooth. Strain and season with salt, cayenne pepper or tabasco sauce and lemon juice. Beat in the remaining butter.

433 VINAIGRETTE SAUCE

3 parts olive oil to 1 part vinegar
salt
freshly ground pepper
herbs, spices, or salad spices

Beat the oil and vinegar together and add seasoning to taste. Be careful with the salt. The sauce can be flavoured with crushed garlic and French mustard.

434 CUSTARD
Serves 4

300 ml/7 fl oz double cream
$^1/_2$ vanilla pod
3 egg yolks
2-3 tbsp sugar

Pour the cream into a heavy-based saucepan. Cut the vanilla pod lengthwise and scrape the seeds into the cream. Add the remaining pod. Bring the cream to the boil and simmer for 3-4 minutes. Remove the pan from the heat and set aside for 15 minutes. Beat the egg yolks and sugar until light and airy and stir the mixture into the cream. Simmer over low heat, beating until thickened. Remove the vanilla pod. Allow the sauce to cool. Keep in a cool place. 100 ml/$3^1/_2$ fl oz double cream may be added just before serving. (Also see recipe 317.

435 CUSTARD CREAM

500 ml/17 fl oz milk
1 vanilla pod
30 g/1 oz flour
85 g/3 oz sugar
$^1/_4$ tsp salt
1 tbsp melted butter
4 eggs
2 egg yolks

Pour the milk into a saucepan. Halve the vanilla pod lengthwise and scrape the seeds into the milk. Add the pod. Bring to the boil and simmer over low heat for 5 minutes. Beat together the eggs, egg yolks, flour, sugar, salt and butter. Beat in the boiling strained milk. Pour the mixture back into the saucepan and bring to the boil, beating vigorously. Set aside to cool, beating occasionally. Keep in the refrigerator until ready to serve.

436 RAW CREAM
Serves 8

2 egg yolks
2 tbsp icing sugar or castor sugar
4 tsp vanilla essence
400 ml/14 fl oz whipping cream

Beat together the egg yolks and sugar. Add the vanilla essence. Beat the cream until it forms stiff peaks and mix with the egg mixture.

437 FLEURONGER
6-8 pieces

1 sheet frozen puff pastry, thawed
1 egg, lightly beaten

Preheat the oven to 250° C/500° F, gas mark 10. Line a baking sheet with greaseproof paper. Brush one side of the pastry with water. Double the sheet over, with the damp sides inwards. Press out crescent shapes. Place the pastry shapes on the baking sheet and brush with the egg. Bake in the oven for 5-6 minutes until the pastry has risen.

438 CHEESE STICKS
approximately 18 sticks

1 frozen puff pastry sheet, thawed
1 egg, beaten
6 tbsp grated Emmental or Gruyère cheese

6 tbsp grated Parmesan cheese
Preheat the oven to 220° C/425° F, gas mark 7. Line a baking sheet with greaseproof paper. Brush the dough with the beaten egg. Mix the two types of cheese together. Sprinkle half the cheese over the pastry sheet and pat down with the palm of the hand. Turn the sheet over, sprinkle over the remaining cheese and pat down. Cut the sheet into 1-cm/ 1/4-inch wide strips from the short side. Twist each strip to make a spiral and place on the baking sheet. Bake the cheese for approximately 8 minutes. These can be made several days in advance but are best freshly baked. Store in a dry place.

439 ORANGE RATAFIAS
approximately 25 biscuits

1 egg
85 g/3 oz castor sugar
100 ml/3 1/2 fl oz melted butter
120 g/4 1/4 oz flour
grated rind of 1 orange

Preheat the oven to 170° C/325° F, gas mark 3. Line a baking sheet with greaseproof paper. Beat the eggs and sugar together until light and fluffy. Add the cold melted butter and the flour alternately. Mix thoroughly. Stir in the orange rind. Spoon teaspoons of the mixture on to the baking sheet and flatten slightly. Bake the biscuits for 5 minutes, until they are golden.

440 FLORENTINES
approximately 30 biscuits

60 g/2 oz almonds, finely chopped
110 g/3 3/4 oz castor sugar
100 g/3 1/2 oz + 2 tsp butter
2 tbsp flour
2 tbsp milk

Preheat the oven to 170° C/325° F, gas mark 3. Grease a baking sheet with 2 tsp of the butter and coat with half the flour. Mix all the remaining ingredients together in a heavy-based saucepan and simmer, stirring. Place small quantities of the mixture on the baking sheet. Space them well apart as they will spread out during baking. Bake the biscuits for 5 minutes, until golden. Allow them to cool slightly on the baking sheet and then remove them with a palette knife. While they are still warm, shape them by bending them over a florentine biscuit iron or a rolling pin.

441 ALMOND RATAFIAS
approximately 40

400 g/14 oz almond paste
2 egg whites
few drops food colouring

Garnish:
red and green cocktail cherries
hazelnuts
walnuts

Preheat the oven to 200° C/400° F, gas mark 6. Line a baking sheet with greaseproof paper. Grate the almond paste and mix with the egg whites until smooth. Colour with 1 or more colours, mixing in the food colouring thoroughly. Pipe the paste on to the baking sheet. Garnish with cocktail cherries or nuts. Bake the ratafias for 8-10 minutes. Lift the paper from the tray with the ratafias still on it. Rinse the baking sheet in ice-cold water, return the ratafias, still on the paper, to the rinsed baking tray. They can then be easily removed without sticking.

442 NUT CAKES
approximately 50

200 g/7 oz + 2 tsp softened butter
130 g/4 1/2 oz castor sugar
120 g/4 1/4 oz hazelnuts, finely chopped
240 g/8 1/2 oz flour

Garnish:
hazelnuts, halved

Preheat the oven to 170° C/325° F, gas mark 3. Grease a baking sheet with 2 tsp of the butter. Mix all the remaining ingredients together until smooth. Pipe or swirl the mixture on to the baking sheet. Garnish with hazelnut halves. Bake the biscuits for approximately 8 minutes.

443 WALNUT FLAKE BISCUITS
approximately 20 biscuits

50 g/1 3/4 oz walnuts, finely chopped
60 g/2 oz castor sugar
50 g/1 3/4 oz butter
1 1/2 tsp flour
1 tbsp milk

Preheat the oven to 170° C/325° F, gas mark 3. Line a baking sheet with greaseproof paper. Mix all the ingredients together in a heavy-based saucepan and simmer, stirring. Divide the mixture into 20 pieces and arrange on the baking sheet, leaving space between each biscuit. The mixture will spread out during baking. Bake the biscuits for approximately 5 minutes until they are golden.

A FEW MENU SUGGESTIONS

SPRING MENUS

Asparagus 195

Gravad Lax and Cucumber Sauce 207

Vanilla Parfait with Raspberry Sauce 397

Chicken Liver Timbale 180

Baked Salmon 221

Fruit and Berry Flan 324

Morel Soup with Smoked Salmon 115

Herby Salt Beef 240

Petits Choux Ring 349

Salmon Plate 163

Wallenberg's Veal Burger 280

Rhubarb Meringue 315

SUMMER MENUS

Matjes Herring Mould 134

Herring 'Sandwiches' 201

Blueberry Pie 322

Sparkling Cucumber Soup 114

Butterfly Salmon with Herb Sauce 213

Pavlova 345

Melon with Parma Ham 182

Stuffed Sea Bass 222

Strawberry Cake 326

Pickled Sherry or Pickled Salt Herrings 137

Regatta Pork Chops 257

Melon with Raspberries and Port 313

Pickled Baltic Herring 135

Ham with Blackcurrant Sauce 261

Quick Raspberry Ice Cream 387

AUTUMN MENUS

Chanterelle Soup 118

Roast Leg of Lamb Provençal 264

Hanna's French Apple Cake 363

Crayfish Mould 153

Juniper Chops 267

Lingonberry Parfait 392

Crayfish Gratinée 147

Fagelfars 285

Blueberry Cake 339

Salmon Tartar 156

Roast Ptarmigan or Grouse Breasts 291

Cloudberry Parfait Cake 388

WINTER MENUS

Crème Ninon 110

Slotts Steak 237

Caramel Custard 361

Cocktail Selection 100

Prawn Soup 117

Roast Venison with Pink Pepper Sauce 268

Ice Cream Meringue 384

Mini Crustades 103

Avocado Soup 108

Lobster Thermidor 150

Pheasant Breast 283

Roast Ptarmigan or Grouse Breast 291

Cheese Board 302

Tropical Fruit Salad 319

Chessboard Cake 107

Vichyssoise 111

Roast Stuffed Turkey 284

Riz à L'Impératrice 366

PARTY MENUS ALL YEAR ROUND

Savoury Petits Choux 104

Halibut with Pepper Sauce 200

Chocolate Cake à la Varennes 338

Pickled Fillet of Beef 175

Fish Mould 203

Baked Pineapple with Passion Fruit 307

Onion Tart 121

Perch or Pike with Chive Sauce 210

Cheese Soufflé 303

Grapefruit Parfait with Toffee Sauce 386

Duck Breast Salad 171

Sole with Prawns 218

Walnut Cake with Coffee Cream 358

Chicken Livers in Aspic 177

Plaice Rolls with Prawns 219

Blackcurrant Sorbet in Almond Baskets 395

Smoked Meat with Cucumber 183

Baked Turbot 220

Cheese Pasties 301

Chocolate Truffles 337

Blinis 131

Beef Stroganov 225

Charlotte Russe 362

Old Man's Mixture 136

Boeuf Bourguignonne 226

Swedish Veiled Country Lass 316

Avocado Soup 108

Entrecôte with Tarragon 227

Sparkling Elderflower Sorbet 394

Mussel Soup 116

Flambéed Fillet of Beef 228

Grand Dessert 306

Canapés 101

Fillet of Beef Provençal 233

Cheese Board 302

Floating Islands 375

Joppe's Prawn Salad 159

Swiss Schnitzel 245

White Chocolate Mousse and Kiwi Sauce 376

Tagliatelle with Salmon Sauce 167

Vitello Tonnato 246

Zabaglione with Berries 321

Avocado Cocktail 187

Pork with Peppercorn Sauce 249

Profiteroles with Toffee Sauce 351

Tomato Salad 199

Nasi Goreng 255

Hawaiian Sandwich 355

Salmon Mousse 154

Kidneys with Mustard Sauce 270

Ice Cream Sandwiches 379

Crudités with Dips 102

Hamburgers 276

'Dime' Bar Ice Cream 378

Ice Cream Ratafia Melba 382

Green Bean Pasty with Chanterelles 194

Duck à L'Orange 281

Raspberry Mousse 371

Ice Cream Truffles 385

Swedish Salad 170

Pheasant Breast 283

Mango Parfait with Strawberry Sauce 393

Snails in Garlic Butter 166

Chicken with Brandy 288

Cinnamon Parfait with Apple Sauce 390

VEGETARIAN MENUS

Broccoli Quiche 119

Aubergine au Gratin 292

Honeyed Bananas 308

Vegetable Pâté with Speckled Sauce 192

Tomato Quiche 295

Frozen Lemon Cake 380

BUFFETS

Salmon Quiche 120

Farmhouse Pâté 181

Cheese Board 302

Tropical Fruit Salad 319

Pickled Baltic Herring 135

Crab Flan with White Sauce 124

Chef's Chicken Salad 294

Cheese Board 302

Chocolate Ratafias 336

Prawn Cake 162
or
Prawn Ring 160

Herby Salt Beef 240

Cheese Pâté 123

Watermelon Basket 320

Shellfish Pâté 164

Gravad Lax 206

Beef Salad 293

Pinocchio Cake 350

Salmon Mould 212

Cheese Flan 122

Tomato Salad 199

Zuleika Cake 359

INDEX